W9-CBR-610

What are

FORCES?

First published in 2018 by Wayland
Copyright © Hodder and Stoughton 2018

Wayland
Carmelite House
50 Victoria Embankment
London EC4Y 0DZ
All rights reserved

Managing editor: Victoria Brooker
Creative design: Paul Cherrill

ISBN: 978 1 5263 0637 1

Printed in China

MIX
Paper from
responsible sources
FSC
www.fsc.org
FSC® C104740

Wayland is a division of
Hachette Children's Books,
an Hachette UK company.
www.hachette.co.uk

What are

FORCES?

Written by
KAY BARNHAM

Illustrated by
MIKE GORDON

WAYLAND

'Come on, Dad!' said Liam.
He danced impatiently around the shopping trolley.
'We've been at the supermarket for *hours*.'
'I just need 27 more things ...' murmured Dad,
looking at his list.
Emma groaned.

4

'I'm joking,' said Dad, with a wink.
He put a tub of ice cream in the shopping trolley
and pushed. Slowly, the trolley began to move
towards the checkouts. 'Let's go!'

'So, why *does* a shopping trolley move?'
Dad asked Liam and Emma, as they loaded
shopping bags into the car.

'Is this a trick question?' Emma said.
'It moves because you push it, right?'
'If you didn't push it,' added Liam,
'the trolley would stay still.'
'That's right!' said Dad.

'When I push the trolley, that's
a force,' explained Dad.
'The force makes the trolley move.
And when something moves,
that's called motion.'

'Look at me!' Liam laughed as he pushed the trolley back to the supermarket. 'I'm using a force!' 'So am I,' said Emma, pushing the boot lid shut with a *bang*. 'You've got it!' said Dad.

9

'There's *another* force that makes things move,' said Dad, when they got home. 'I'll give you a clue. It's the opposite to a push ...'

Emma pulled the front door open. Then she froze. 'I know!' she cried. 'A *pull* is a force!'

'When it's snowy, I pull my sledge up the hill!' Liam grinned.

Dad gave them both a high five. 'Brilliant,' he said.

'There you are!' said Mum, pushing back her chair and pulling the children into a group hug. 'I hope you didn't buy *too* many treats.'

'Of course not,' said Dad. He pulled
open the freezer door and pushed the tub
of ice cream inside. 'We were too busy
talking about forces and motion.'
'Great!' said Mum. 'Then come outside!'

Mum pulled the scooter out of the shed.
'What happens if you scoot forward
and I push you?' she asked the children.
'I'll go faster!' said Emma.

Mum nodded. 'If a force happens in the same direction the object is moving, that object speeds up.'
'Let's do it now!' said Liam.

'So what happens if
a force happens in the opposite
direction?' asked Emma.
'Think of the scooter again,'
said Mum. 'If you were scooting
and I pulled you backwards,
what would happen then?'

'Emma would go slower,'
said Liam.
'And if I pulled hard
enough, she'd stop,'
added Mum.

The next day, Mum, Dad and Liam
went to watch Emma play football.
'Look what happens when the ball is moving
and then another player kicks it,' said Dad.

'The ball goes a different way!' said Liam.
'That's because a kick is a force,' said Mum.
'When an object is moving in a straight line,
a force can change its direction.'

A player kicked the ball and it rolled off the pitch towards them. It slowed and then stopped in front of Liam. One of the players came to get it.

'So why did the ball slow down?' asked Liam. 'It wasn't pushed or pulled.' 'Aha,' said Mum. 'It was because of friction.'

'What's friction?' asked Liam, as
Emma joined them. The match was over.
'Friction is a force that happens when one
object slides across another object,' explained
Dad. 'Friction makes an object go slower.'
'The ball is sliding across the grass,' said Mum.
'But the grass slows it down.

'Rough objects have more friction than smooth objects,' said Dad. 'Grass is rough, so it causes more friction than something smooth.'
'Like ice?' asked Emma.

'Exactly,' said Dad. 'Ice is very smooth.
It's easier to slide across ice because there is
less friction. It would be much more difficult for
an ice skater to skate across a football pitch.'
Emma spluttered with laughter.

They all cycled home.
Emma and Liam had fun speeding up,
slowing down and changing direction.
Their parents had to pedal hard to keep up.

'Hey!' Emma called over her shoulder to Mum
and Dad. 'We've had a brilliant idea!'
'Follow us!' shouted Liam, heading into the park.

'I don't see what's brilliant about this idea,'
grumbled Dad, a few minutes later.
'Me neither,' said Mum, puffing and panting.
'It's genius!' Liam laughed. 'We've learned all
about forces and motion today ...'

'... so pushing us on the swings is the perfect way to celebrate,' finished Emma. 'Pushing is a force. And look ... we're in motion!' 'Wheeeeeeeee!' cried the children as they soared through the air.

NOTES FOR PARENTS AND TEACHERS

The aim of this book is to introduce children to scientific concepts in an entertaining, informative way. Here are some ideas for activities that will encourage them to think further about forces — and have fun doing it!

ACTIVITIES

1. How many different examples can you think of pushing and pulling?
2. Draw a diagram of something like a car or a bicycle moving faster, slower and changing direction. Use arrows to show the direction of the forces that act upon this object.
3 Can you rearrange these anagrams to find 5 phrases to do with forces and motion?

HUG PINS

GILL PUN

IT MOON

RIFT COIN

FRESCO

PUSHING, PULLING, MOTION, FRICTION, FORCES

FORCES EXPERIMENT

You will need:
• table tennis balls
• straws
• a friend

Put the table tennis ball on a smooth surface. Now blow air through straws to demonstrate how forces work.

If you blow air steadily at a ball, it will move in a straight line.

If you blow harder, the ball will speed up.

If your friend blows from the opposite direction, the ball will slow down.

If your friend blows from the side, the ball will change direction!

If you put the ball on to a rough surface like the carpet, watch how friction affects the motion of the ball. It will move much more slowly!

DID YOU KNOW ...?

Gravity is a force that pulls objects — including houses, schools, cars and you — towards Earth.

Springs and elastic bands are made of materials that want to stay the same shape. If a spring is squashed or an elastic band is stretched, their elastic force makes them go back to their original shape.

Forces are measured in newtons. The unit was named after the famous scientist Sir Isaac Newton (1642–1727) who studied forces and motion.

BOOKS TO SHARE

Forces
(*Boom Science* series)
by Georgia Amson-Bradshaw
(Watts Publishing, 2018)

Forces and Magnets
(*Fact Cat* series)
by Izzi Powell
(Wayland, 2018)

Forces
(*Outdoor Science* series)
by Izzi Howell
(Wayland, 2018)

Forces and Magnets
(*Moving up with Science* series)
by Peter Riley
(Watts Publishing, 2016)